Then and Now

Life at Work

Vicki Yates

Heinemann
LIBRARY
Chicago, Illinois

© 2008 Heinemann Library
a division of Reed Elsevier Inc.
Chicago, Illinois

Customer Service 888-454-2279
Visit our website at www.heinemannraintree.com

Designed by Victoria Bevan and Joanna Hinton-Malivoire
Photo research by Ruth Smith and Q2A Solutions
Printed and bound in China by South China Printing Co. Ltd.

12 11 10 09 08
10 9 8 7 6 5 4 3 2 1

ISBN-10: 1-4034-9834-2 (hc)   1-4034-9842-3 (pb)

The Library of Congress has cataloged the first edition of this book as follows:
Yates, Vicki.
  Life at work / Vicki Yates.
     p. cm. -- (Then and now)
  Includes bibliographical references and index.
  ISBN-13: 978-1-4034-9834-2 (hc)
  ISBN-13: 978-1-4034-9842-7 (pb)
 1. Occupations--Juvenile literature. 2. Occupations--History--Juvenile literature. 3. Work--Juvenile literature. 4. Work--History--
Juvenile literature. I. Title.
  HF5381.2.Y38 2008
  331--dc22

2579   2007014732

Acknowledgements
Bionikmedia p. **22**; Collections of The Historical Society of Princeton p. **18**; Corbis pp. **10** (Baldwin H. Ward & Kathryn C. Ward),
12 (EFE), **13** (Left Lane Productions) **15** (Jonny Le Fortune/Zefa); Enco p. **11** (Jan Napieralski, Poland); Ford Media p. **21**; GM
Motors p. **20**; Harcourt Index p. **4**; John Deere p. **9**; Library of Congress p. **14**; New York Picture Library p. **6**; Photolibrary.
com pp. **16**, **17** (Index Stock Imagery), **19** (Photo Researchers, Inc); Science & Society Picture Library p. **5** (Colin T Gifford);
Shutterstock p. **23**; Staffordshire County Records Office pp. **8**, **23**; Valtra Media p. **7**, **23**.

Cover photographs reproduced with permission of Corbis: farmer (Bettmanfarmern), tractor (Lester Lefkowitz).
Back cover photograph reproduced with permission of GM Motors.

Contents

What Is work?

Work is the jobs people do.
People have jobs to make money.

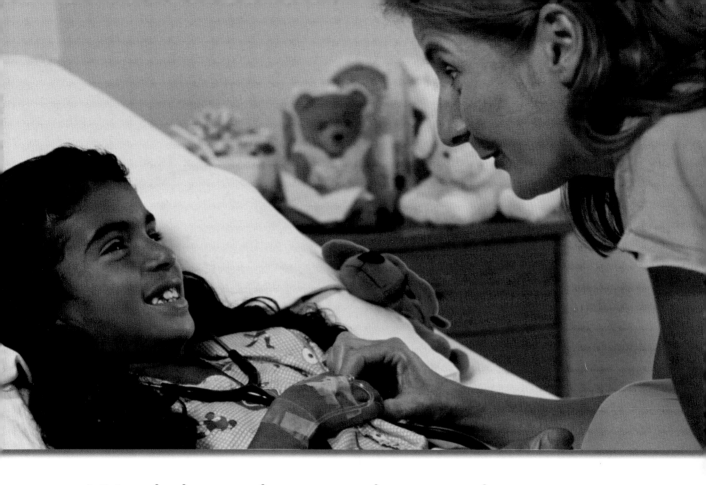

Work has changed over the years.

Different Jobs

plow

Long ago farmers used a horse and plow.

Today farmers can use a tractor and plow.

Long ago builders used small tools.

Today builders can use big machines.

Long ago people made clothes
by hand.

Today people can make clothes
with machines.

Long ago people counted money in their heads.

Today people count money
with machines.

Long ago people wrote with typewriters.

Today people write with
computers.

Long ago doctors saw people at home.

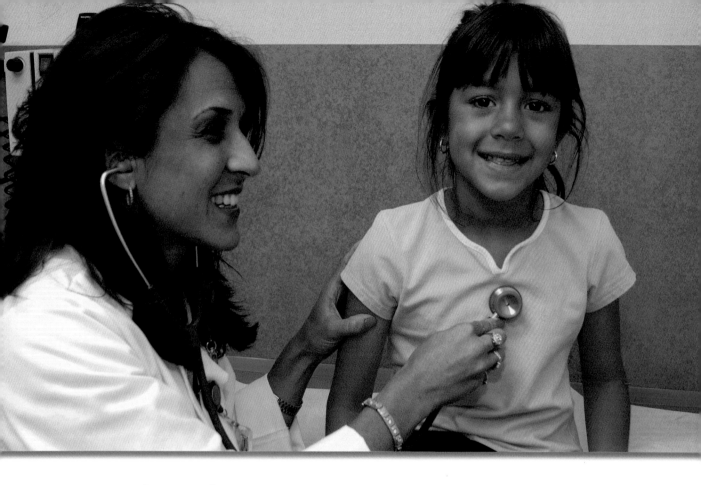

Today doctors see people in an office.

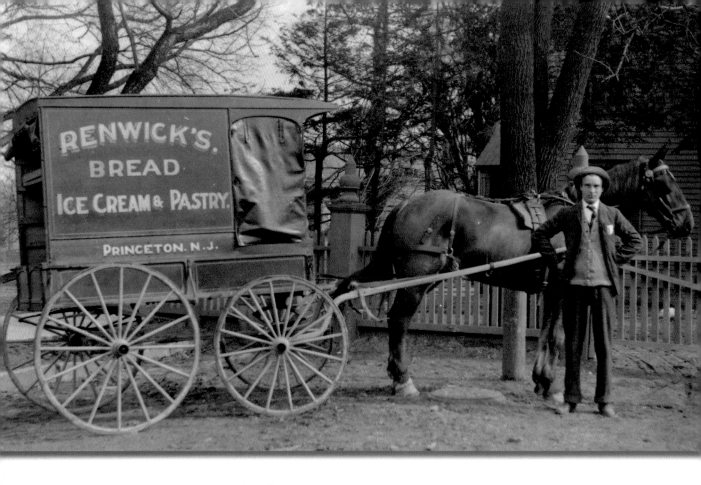

Long ago delivery drivers used horses and wagons.

Today delivery drivers use trucks.

Let's Compare

Long ago people worked to make a living.

Today people still work to make a living.

Who Are They?

What job do these men do?

Answer on p. 24

Picture Glossary

money coins or bills that people use to buy things

plow a machine that farmers use to turn over soil

tool something that helps you do a job

Index

Answer to question on p. 22: They are firemen.

Note to Parents and Teachers
Before reading: Ask children what jobs they would like to do when they are older. What jobs do their parents do? What time do their parents go to work?

After reading: Using the book, ask children to look through the images from the past and discuss how work has changed. Discuss with children elements of work life that have remained the same.

You can support children's nonfiction literacy skills by helping them use the table of contents, headings, picture glossary, and index.

JAN   2008